SNAPSHOTS IN HISTORY

THE NEW DEAL

Rebuilding America

by Stephanie Fitzgerald

THE NEW DEAL

Rebuilding America

by Stephanie Fitzgerald

Content Adviser: Derek Shouba, Adjunct History Professor
and Assistant Provost, Roosevelt University

Reading Adviser: Katie Van Sluys, Ph.D.,
School of Education, DePaul University

COMPASS POINT BOOKS
MINNEAPOLIS, MINNESOTA

COMPASS POINT BOOKS

3109 West 50th Street, #115
Minneapolis, MN 55410

Visit Compass Point Books on the Internet at
www.compasspointbooks.com
or e-mail your request to
custserv@compasspointbooks.com

For Compass Point Books
Jennifer VanVoorst, Jaime Martens, XNR Productions, Inc.,
Catherine Neitge, Keith Griffin, and Carol Jones

Produced by White-Thomson Publishing Ltd.

For White-Thomson Publishing
Stephen White-Thomson, Susan Crean, Amy Sparks,
Tinstar Design Ltd., Derek Shouba, Peggy Bresnick Kendler,
Laurel Haines, and Timothy Griffin

Library of Congress Cataloging-in-Publication Data
Fitzgerald, Stephanie.
  The New Deal : Rebuilding America / by Stephanie Fitzgerald.
    p. cm. — (Snapshots in history)
  Includes bibliographical references and index.
  ISBN-13: 978-0-7565-2096-0 (hardcover)
  ISBN-10: 0-7565-2096-7 (hardcover)
  1. United States—History—1933–1945—Juvenile literature. 2. United
States—History—1919–1933—Juvenile literature. 3. New Deal, 1933–
1939—Juvenile literature. 4. Roosevelt, Franklin D. (Franklin Delano),
1882–1945—Juvenile literature. 5. Depressions—1929—United
States—Juvenile literature. 6. United States—Economic conditions—
1918–1945—Juvenile literature. I. Title. II. Series.
  E806.F5 2007
  973.917—dc22   2006008395

CONTENTS

A New Hope

President Franklin Delano Roosevelt's inauguration day was cold, gray, and rainy. It was a day that matched the economic and emotional state of the country. The inauguration took place on March 4, 1933, almost four months after Roosevelt had won the election. The United States was in the suffocating grip of the Great Depression. Families were homeless, and children were starving. For many, it seemed that all was lost.

For four years, Americans had been living under these conditions with a president who they felt was doing nothing to help them. No matter how bad things got, Republican President Herbert Hoover seemed to refuse to give people what he called "handouts." He practically refused to even admit there was a problem.

As people's daily lives worsened, Hoover continued to tell them things were really improving. Radios only played happy songs, and theaters showed humorous movies—as if that would make people forget their terrible situation.

But Roosevelt defeated Hoover to become the 32nd president of the United States. On the Saturday of Roosevelt's inauguration, there was a new feeling of optimism in the country. Hope was replacing despair. Despite the terrible weather, 500,000 people came to watch Roosevelt's inaugural parade. The area in front of the U.S. Capitol was filled with 100,000 people who waited to hear the new president deliver his inaugural address.

Franklin Roosevelt and his wife, Eleanor, were the focus of the inaugural parade in March 1933.

Millions more Americans listened at home. When Roosevelt spoke, he offered the promise of hope and a bold course of action. He told the American people:

> *This great nation will endure as it has endured, will revive, and will prosper. So, first of all, let me assert my firm belief that the only thing we have to fear is fear itself— nameless, unreasoning, unjustified terror, which paralyzes needed efforts to convert retreat into advance. In every dark hour of our national life a leadership of frankness and vigor has met with that understanding and support of the people themselves, which is essential to victory. I am convinced that you will again give that support to leadership in these critical days.*

> *The people of the United States have not failed. In their need they have registered a mandate that they want direct, vigorous action. They have asked for discipline and direction under leadership. They have made me the present instrument of their wishes. In the spirit of the gift, I take it.*

Roosevelt's speech inspired confidence in the American people. When he first announced his candidacy for president, however, he seemed to many to be an unlikely candidate. Although Roosevelt had been in politics for more than 20 years, many people did not see him as a very serious politician.

THE ONLY THING WE HAVE TO FEAR IS FEAR ITSELF--

1933

MARCH 4, 1933

Millions of Americans listened to Roosevelt's inaugural speech on their radios at home.

Roosevelt had been a state senator and assistant secretary of the U.S. Navy. Most recently, he had been the governor of New York. Even so, he had done very little to make a name for himself in politics. Roosevelt was a charming, sociable, and popular man. People thought the only reason he had made it in politics was because he came from a wealthy family. He did not seem to be a likely person to rescue the United States from the worst economic disaster in the nation's history.

11

But Americans were desperate for a change. After three long years, it seemed like an end to the Great Depression was nowhere in sight. Even though President Hoover promised the American people that things would improve, the situation was going from bad to worse. Every day, more businesses failed, more people lost their jobs, and more children went hungry. To many, it seemed as if Hoover had no real plan to end the Depression.

From the moment Roosevelt announced his candidacy, he represented a breath of fresh air to those suffering. Roosevelt promised a "new deal" for the United States. He promised to look after the forgotten people, and there was hardly anyone in the United States at the time who did not feel that he or she was forgotten. Finally there was a presidential candidate who was promising real help. Someone had a plan to end the Depression.

Roosevelt captured the country's attention—first with the speech he gave when he decided to run for president, and again with the campaign that took him all across the country. Americans often gathered by the thousands wherever Roosevelt appeared to

STEPPING STONE TO SUCCESS

During his time as governor, Roosevelt had established a Temporary Emergency Relief Administration (TERA) in New York. The program was funded by the government and by a state tax increase. Although the program could only scratch the surface of economic problems, it was the biggest state program in the country. Voters across the United States did not know what Roosevelt was doing in New York, but his actions showed other members of the Democratic Party that he had a plan for economic recovery.

President Roosevelt was joined by his wife, Eleanor, and son James as they prepared to move into the White House after the inauguration.

campaign, and they showed their support at the polls, too. When Roosevelt was elected in November 1932, people across the country hoped he could work a miracle.

President Roosevelt knew he had a huge battle to fight, and he knew he had to act quickly. He would not disappoint. In the first 100 days of his presidency, Roosevelt instituted 15 programs that focused on relief, recovery, and reform. These programs would form the basis of what would be called the New Deal. It was the first time in U.S. history that the federal government would take such an active role in organizing private businesses and agriculture. It was also the first time the government would be directly involved in the lives of individual citizens. No president before or since accomplished so much in so little time. ◣

13

From Boom to Bust

Chapter

2

President Roosevelt's election quickly lifted the nation's spirits. People finally believed the end of the Depression was in sight. At the very least, they had a president who was willing to address the problem. In reality, the fight to end the Depression would take a long time. The economic crash had been in the making for more than five years. It would take at least as long to turn things around.

During the nation's participation in the final two years of World War I (1914–1918), the United States experienced a real boom. Farmers supplied extra food to European allies, and factories created war materials used in the fighting. As a result, there were plenty of jobs to go around.

Once the war ended, however, farmers had more crops than they could possibly sell. Factories stopped making war materials, so fewer jobs were available. And once U.S. soldiers came back from fighting, there were even more people competing for those few jobs.

Factory production of weapons during World War I helped the U.S. economy remain strong.

15

Despite the economic slowdown, the United States appeared to be the richest country in the world in the 1920s. At that time, Americans believed that spending—not saving—their money was the best way to get rich, as well as the best way to keep the nation's economy going strong.

WORLDWIDE CRISIS

The United States was not the only country affected by the end of World War I. As the loser, Germany was forced to pay billions of dollars in war reparations to the Allies, mainly to Great Britain and France. As a result, Germany's economy took a dive. Germany's financial problems dragged down other European countries, too.

In fact, it was almost considered unpatriotic for people to keep their money in the bank. People thought that the more they spent, the better businesses would do, which meant more jobs for more workers. It also meant more taxes were collected to keep the country running smoothly.

People were spending money on all kinds of luxuries such as new cars and homes, electrical appliances, and fancy clothes. This was the first time that many of these items were affordable enough for middle-class people to purchase. Unfortunately, people were using money they did not really have to buy these things.

A new way of shopping had become popular: buying on an installment plan. If something cost $10, a person could purchase it with $1 cash and then pay the rest of the money over time by making a payment once a month. Using this system, people felt they could afford anything they wanted. They did not worry about how they would pay for their purchases every month.

This new way of buying made it so that anyone could live like a wealthy person. Many people thought they could use this type of plan to become wealthy for real. If they could buy stocks on an installment plan, they thought, they might really be able to strike it rich.

By buying on installment plans, many women in the 1920s dressed like movie stars, even though they could not really afford to.

Buying on margin gave people the chance to do just that. This meant a person could buy stocks through a broker. The person would put down 10 percent of the cost, and the broker would pay the difference. At the time, stock prices were rising so fast that people really did have the chance to make a fortune.

Unfortunately, no one thought about what would happen if the prices went down. Then, when a broker wanted to be repaid the other 90 percent, the buyer would have to come up with that cash. People did not think that far ahead, however, because they did not think prices would ever go down.

American people were living as if the good times would never end. However, even before the stock market crashed in 1929, there were signs that things were changing for the worse.

The United States had lost more than 120,000 soldiers and spent billions of dollars during World War I. By the time the war ended, most Americans did not want anything to do with

INVESTING IN THE STOCK MARKET

Selling stock, or shares of ownership in a company, to outside investors is a good way for a business to grow. Investors buy and sell shares of stock in what is called the stock market. These transactions happen at the New York Stock Exchange, where brokers buy and sell stocks for their customers, the investors. When the value of each piece of stock increases, investors can make money by selling their shares for more money than they paid for them. When the value goes down, investors will lose money if they sell the stock for less than they paid for it. Every time people buy stocks, they are taking a risk. There are no guarantees that the stocks will increase in value.

the rest of the world. They adopted an isolationist attitude toward politics and trade.

American workers were concerned that they would lose their jobs if people were buying foreign goods. To keep foreign-made products out of the United States, the government placed a very high tax, called a tariff, on all foreign goods imported into the country. This resulted in a trade war. As the United States placed a tariff on foreign products, the Europeans responded by placing a similar tax on American-made products imported into their countries. As a result, American exports were cut in half, which led to more Americans losing their jobs.

Although attitudes at the end of World War I led to financial problems for the United States, it was not until years later that the Great Depression officially began. Today, most people point to the stock market crash of 1929 as the start of the Great Depression.

The U.S. stock market had been experiencing steady growth, but it began slipping downward on Monday, October 21, 1929. Once stock prices started dropping, brokers advised their clients to sell their shares. There were so many sales that day that people started to panic. The stock prices and market activity were reported on the radio and in the newspapers. Once people heard that others were selling their shares, they thought they should sell theirs, too.

More and more people started telling their brokers that they wanted to sell. Two days later, the stock market experienced its busiest trading day ever. More than $4 billion was lost in one day.

Three days later, stock prices plummeted. October 24, 1929, later became known as Black Thursday. No one was ready for what happened that day. In order to pay for their customers' margin loans, brokers had taken loans of their own from banks. On Black Thursday, the banks called in their loans. The brokers, in turn, called their customers

On Black Thursday, people crowded Wall Street, home to the New York Stock Exchange, as they waited for news about the stock market.

and demanded that they pay off their debts. When customers could not pay or could not be reached, brokers sold their stocks—often at a loss. Then they used the money to pay off their own debts. Many investors lost all of their stocks—and their entire life savings—in one terrible morning.

That same day, five of the biggest bankers in the United States decided to step in and try to stop the panic. They pooled their money and started buying stocks. They wanted investors to see that not everyone was selling. This slowed the initial panic, but not for long.

The next Monday, October 28, 1929, stock prices raced downward and never stopped. Within weeks, millions of Americans lost a total of $30 billion—the equivalent of about $340 billion in today's dollars. It was the worst financial disaster in the history of the United States.

The collapse of the stock market created a domino effect throughout the nation. Investors lost their money—both the money they put down to buy the stocks and the money they still owed their brokers. When brokers could not pay off their bank loans, banks had to close. When people saw that banks were closing, they panicked. They hurried to take their money out, causing banks that were not originally in trouble to close, too. Now, even if people had money in the bank, they could not get it. Worse yet, they would probably never see it again.

$100. WILL BUY THIS CAR. MUST HAVE CASH. LOST ALL ON THE STOCK MARKET

Small businesses that had invested in banks that closed down had to close their doors, too. This led to people losing their jobs. Even the businesses that stayed open had to lay off workers. Nobody had money to spend on the companies' products, so they could not afford to pay many workers.

Banks that were in trouble also had to call in mortgages, the loans they made to homeowners and farmers. If the customer could not make a mortgage payment, the bank could foreclose on the loan, or take that person's property and sell it.

Before long, signs of despair were evident everywhere. Wealthy men who had lost their

After the stock market crashed, people who had lost everything tried to raise money any way they could.

fortunes in the stock market collapse committed suicide. Others had mental breakdowns and had to be placed in institutions.

People who had worked hard all their lives and saved their money now saw their jobs and their life savings disappear. People who had no money scrounged in garbage cans for food and collected wood by the roadside to keep warm. Workers showed up at warehouses, loading docks, and construction sites, hoping to get hired for the day.

Some families had to send their children away to relatives when they could no longer pay for heat or electricity. Sometimes, families lost their homes entirely. Some families were even forced to live in cardboard boxes and rusted-out cars.

Countless Americans sought help to find jobs through employment agencies during the Depression.

BUYING THE FARM

When people buy property, whether it is a home or a farm, they pay part of the purchase price up front and take out a mortgage for the rest. Then they make a mortgage payment to the bank every month to pay off the loan over a number of years. During the Depression, many farmers were not able to make their monthly mortgage payments. When this happened, the bank would come in, force the farmers off their land, and sell it. It did not matter how much or how little the farmer still owed. Often when a farm was sold, so was everything on it, from livestock to machinery to family photos and memorabilia.

Times were hard everywhere, from the cities to the farms. At the height of the Depression, as much as 25 percent of the entire workforce, or as many as 16 million people, were unemployed. Between 1930 and 1935, more than 750,000 farms were lost through foreclosure.

People were desperate. Those who could not get help from their relatives had to turn to local charities to survive. Bread lines and soup kitchens sprang up everywhere. Peggy Terry, who was a child during the Depression, recalled how these services helped keep her and her sister alive:

> *I first noticed the difference when we'd come home from school in the evening. My mother'd send us to the soup line. ... If you happened to be one of the first ones in line, you didn't get anything but the water that was on top. ... Then we'd go across the street. One place had bread, large loaves of bread. Down the road just a little piece was a big shed, and they gave milk. ... And that's what we lived off for the longest time. ... I can remember one time, the only thing in the house to eat was mustard. My sister and I put so much mustard on biscuits that we got sick. And we can't stand mustard till today.*

Business groups also tried to help unemployed people get back to work. Toward the end of 1930, the International Apple Shippers Association devised a plan to keep their apples from going to waste and help the unemployed at the same time. The association sold the apples to sellers who in turn sold them for 5 cents apiece. That way, the person selling the fruit made a few cents on each apple before paying back the supplier.

The image of jobless men selling apples on the street became a symbol of the Great Depression.

UNEMPLOYED
BUY
APPLES
5¢ EACH

By the end of the year, there were 6,000 people selling apples on the streets of New York City alone.

Local governments, charities, and some businesses did their best to help as many people as they could. But they just did not have the resources to combat a problem this extensive. They needed the help of the federal government.

Unfortunately, President Herbert Hoover refused to lend a hand. Hoover, who had been orphaned as a child, was truly a picture of the American dream: He became rich by working hard. Hoover believed a big part of that dream was allowing individuals to get ahead on their own, without the interference of the government. Hoover warned:

MAKING A NAME FOR HIMSELF

Many of the American people blamed President Hoover for their economic troubles. Though he had not caused the Depression, he was not doing much to help alleviate it. Soon his name became linked to many symbols of the era. Shantytowns where homeless people lived in cardboard boxes or burned out cars became known as Hoovervilles. The newspapers that homeless people used to keep warm were called Hoover blankets. Empty pants pockets that were turned inside out were called Hoover flags.

> *If you let the federal government help the individual, soon the federal government will control that individual.*

The idea of letting people help themselves may have worked during normal times, but drastic times called for drastic measures. Americans were not suffering because they were too lazy to help themselves. They were suffering because the economy had collapsed—and only the federal government could fix it.

27

President Herbert Hoover (center) was a self-made millionaire who believed every person had a shot at the American dream.

Hoover was willing to give financial aid—but only to businesses. He asked Congress to create the Reconstruction Finance Corporation to lend large amounts of money to banks, railroads, and other businesses that were in trouble. Hoover felt that helping the businesses would give the economy a jumpstart and eventually lead to jobs.

Even so, Hoover did little to help common people. In 1932, a group of World War I veterans marched to Washington, D.C., and set up a Hooverville, or shantytown, near the Capitol. They had come to request early payment of the bonus that had been promised to them for fighting in the war, which was not due to be paid until 1945. The crowd, which grew to 20,000 people, was disappointed when the Senate voted down a bill to provide early payment, but they did not cause trouble.

Hoover nevertheless ordered the U.S. Army into the marchers' camp with tanks, bayonets, and tear gas. Many veterans and their families were injured, and their camp was burned to the ground. Hoover's harsh reaction to the bonus marchers further soured his reputation.

By the time of the 1932 presidential election, the United States was three years into the Depression. Americans had had enough. They were looking for someone to save them—and the country—from total ruin.

Although they knew he could not win, the Republican Party let Hoover run for reelection. Had they chosen another candidate, it would have appeared that they were admitting responsibility for the Depression. Hoover ran as the Republican candidate, and his Democratic opponent was New York Governor Franklin Delano Roosevelt. ◼

A New Deal for the American People

Chapter

3

Franklin Delano Roosevelt was born on January 30, 1882, in Hyde Park, New York. His family was very wealthy, and he enjoyed trips to Europe, private tutors, and the most expensive private schools. After graduating from Harvard College, Roosevelt attended Columbia Law School. At the age of 23, he married Eleanor Roosevelt, a distant cousin and the niece of former President Theodore Roosevelt.

Roosevelt entered politics in 1910 when he was elected to the New York Senate. Three years later, he was appointed assistant secretary of the U.S. Navy. Despite these successes, few people considered Roosevelt a serious politician. They thought he was handsome and charming, but they considered him a political lightweight incapable of making any sweeping changes.

In fact, some people joked that the initials FDR could stand for "Feather Duster" Roosevelt.

In 1921, Roosevelt's charmed life took a terrible turn. At age 39, he was struck with infantile paralysis, a type of polio that usually affects children. This infectious disease attacked Roosevelt's spinal cord, and he almost died. Many people, including his mother, wanted Roosevelt to retire from public life.

As a young man, Franklin Delano Roosevelt (bottom row, second from left) played on his high school football team.

Instead, with his wife's encouragement, Roosevelt spent two years in Georgia at what is now called the Roosevelt Warm Springs Institute for Rehabilitation. While there, he swam, worked on his upper body strength, and learned to deal with his paralysis. He even managed to get on his feet again. The physical therapy was grueling, but Roosevelt never gave up. He later said:

> *If you have spent two years in bed trying to wiggle your big toe, everything else seems easy.*

Roosevelt recovered much of his strength during years of physical therapy in Warm Springs, Georgia.

EYES AND EARS

Eleanor Roosevelt, a well-loved and respected leader in her own right, was born in New York City on October 11, 1884. From the time she was a young girl, Eleanor always felt sympathy for the poor and underprivileged. Roosevelt called her his eyes and ears, because Eleanor went to places that his disability kept him from visiting. She started the practice when Roosevelt was governor of New York and continued it after he was elected president. In the first year of Roosevelt's presidency, Eleanor traveled all around the country visiting ordinary Americans and reporting back to the president. She saw firsthand how miners, migrant workers, and the unemployed were living. She talked with people in bread lines and soup kitchens. Eleanor shared all of these stories with her husband so that he would know for himself how the Depression was affecting the American people.

Despite his hard work and progress, Roosevelt would be physically challenged for the rest of his life. In order to walk, he would always need the assistance of leg braces, a cane, and someone to lean on. Nevertheless, Roosevelt emerged from Warm Springs a changed man—and not just physically. His painful struggle to overcome paralysis had matured him. Roosevelt was more sympathetic to the hardships of others, and he was much more interested in and serious about the world around him. In 1928, he was elected governor of New York. Just four years later, he had his eye on the presidency of the United States.

Once Roosevelt decided to run for president, his first task was to convince the Democratic Party that he was the right person for them to back in the 1932 presidential election. When

Roosevelt received the Democratic nomination on the fourth ballot at the party convention, he accepted the nomination in a most unusual way.

At that time, a candidate traditionally waited to accept his nomination until party representatives officially told him of the nomination and asked for his acceptance. But Roosevelt broke with this tradition and flew from Albany, the capital of New York, to the Democratic National Convention in Chicago. There, he accepted the nomination immediately and in person.

The fact that he had to fly through stormy weather to get to Chicago only added to the drama of his unusual acceptance. The way Roosevelt accepted the nomination impressed the convention delegates and got them excited about his candidacy.

Roosevelt's acceptance speech was heard on radios across the country and excited party delegates and the American people alike. He made it clear that he was a strong alternative to President Hoover. What he said that day showed listeners that Roosevelt was a man of action. He talked about creating

DEMOCRATS AND REPUBLICANS

The two major political parties in the United States are the Republicans and the Democrats. The ideals of each party should not be oversimplified, because the beliefs and opinions of party members can vary as much as the members themselves. However, in general, Republicans believe that each individual is responsible for his or her own success. They do not believe the government should interfere in the economic lives of individual citizens. Democrats, on the other hand, often believe that it is up to the government to help when people are in need.

an administration that understood the needs of ordinary people. He promised to create employment programs, help refinance expensive mortgages, and reopen international trade. Roosevelt said that he understood that the American people wanted jobs and a sense of personal and financial security. He

Roosevelt flew to Chicago to accept the Democratic nomination for the presidency in person.

35

said that these were his goals, too. He concluded with a promise:

> *I pledge you, I pledge myself, to a new deal for the American people. Give me your help, not to win votes alone, but to win this crusade to restore America to its own people.*

Roosevelt won far more electoral votes than Hoover did in the 1932 election.

Americans responded to Roosevelt's promises and his pleas by casting 57.3 percent of their votes for him in the November 1932 election. Roosevelt won 472 electoral votes compared to Hoover's 59.

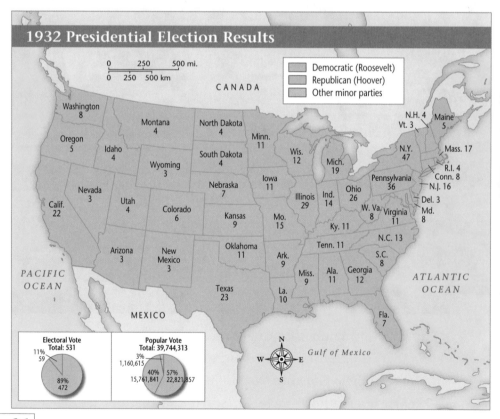

1932 Presidential Election Results

Democratic (Roosevelt)
Republican (Hoover)
Other minor parties

CANADA

Washington 8
Montana 4
North Dakota 4
Minn. 11
N.H. 4
Vt. 3
Maine 5
Oregon 5
Idaho 4
South Dakota 4
Wis. 12
Mich. 19
N.Y. 47
Mass. 17
Wyoming 3
Iowa
Pennsylvania 36
R.I. 4
Conn. 8
N.J. 16
Nevada 3
Nebraska 7
Illinois 29
Ind. 14
Ohio 26
Del. 3
Calif. 22
Utah 4
Colorado 6
Kansas 9
Mo. 15
W. Va. 8
Virginia 11
Md. 8
Ky. 11
N.C. 13
Arizona 3
New Mexico 3
Oklahoma 11
Ark. 9
Tenn. 11
S.C. 8
Miss. 9
Ala. 11
Georgia 12
Texas 23
La. 10
Fla. 7

PACIFIC OCEAN
ATLANTIC OCEAN
MEXICO
Gulf of Mexico

0 250 500 mi.
0 250 500 km

Electoral Vote Total: 531
11% 59
89% 472

Popular Vote Total: 39,744,313
3% 1,160,615
40% 15,761,841
57% 22,821,857

But there was little time to celebrate victory. A huge job lay ahead for the president-elect and his team of advisers. They had to develop their plan for economic recovery.

Complicating matters was the fact that Roosevelt would not officially take office until his inauguration in March of the next year. For about four months, the United States would have a new president who was completely powerless. The country would also have to wait for Hoover, who would be able to accomplish even less than he had before, to leave office. For these four months, the outgoing president was known as a lame duck, because he had no power.

Roosevelt kept busy in the run-up to the inauguration. He had assembled a team of advisers led by three professors from Columbia University— Raymond Moley, Adolf A. Berle, and Rexford G. Tugwell. This group came to be known as Roosevelt's Brain Trust. All of the men on Roosevelt's team supported legislation to help the less-fortunate. They also believed in the need for a strong federal government that would actively plan to end the Depression. By the time Roosevelt took office, the Brain Trust had designed an overall plan for recovery.

THE 20TH AMENDMENT

In 1933, the 20th Amendment to the U.S. Constitution was ratified to correct the long lame-duck period between the election in November and when the new president took office. Since then, a newly elected president enters the office on January 20 in the year following the election.

The Brain Trust, (from left) Raymond Moley, Adolf Berle, and Rexford Tugwell, were Roosevelt's core advisers in the early days of his presidency.

When inauguration day arrived on March 4, 1933, the new president was prepared to take action. Since 1930, the nation's banking system had been shutting down. In fact, between the November election and inauguration day, 12 states had closed a total of more than 5,000 banks. On March 4, the New York Stock Exchange even closed down.

Roosevelt's inaugural speech convinced the people of the United States that he was ready to get to work. His actions confirmed that fact. On Sunday, March 5, 1933, his first full day in office, Roosevelt called the U.S. Congress into special session to take place on Thursday, March 9.

At 1 A.M. on Monday, March 6, he issued a proclamation ordering a bank holiday. All banks were ordered to close for four days. During that time, those banks that could be saved would be reorganized and then reopened. Those banks that could not be saved would close their doors forever.

Meanwhile, Roosevelt's administration worked feverishly to draw up the Emergency Banking Bill. Congress took just four hours to enact it. It was evident that many banks in the United States had failed because of unethical practices. Some banks had invested depositors' money unwisely and sometimes dishonestly. Thanks to the Emergency Banking Bill, the government would regulate all banking procedures in the future.

On March 12, 1933, Roosevelt made a radio address to tell the American people his plans for the country. Millions of people tuned in to hear him speak. The president explained in clear and simple terms why so many banks had failed and why he had declared the bank holiday. Then he talked about what Congress was doing to ensure that such a banking crisis would not happen again.

As he finished his address, Roosevelt talked about the role of each individual in the process:

> *I can assure you, my friends, that it is safer to keep your money in a reopened bank than it is to keep it under the mattress. ... The success of our whole national program depends, of course, on the cooperation of the public—on its intelligent support and its use of a reliable system. ... After all, there is an element in the readjustment of our financial system more important than currency, more important than gold, and that is the confidence of the people themselves.*

President Roosevelt was the first politician to make frequent use of radio addresses.

Confidence and courage are the essentials of success in carrying out our plan. You people must have faith; you must not be stampeded by rumors or guesses. Let us unite in banishing fear. We have provided the machinery to restore our financial system, and it is up to you to support and make it work.

It is your problem, my friends, your problem no less than it is mine. Together we cannot fail.

Roosevelt and his administration had accomplished quite a bit during the two weeks following his inauguration. The members of Congress who had been in Washington, D.C., since December were ready to take a break and go home. But the president was not ready to stop working. He kept Congress in session until mid-June—for 100 days—working out one program after another and laying the foundation of what came to be known as the first New Deal. In order to get the nation back on its feet, these programs would focus on the three R's—relief, recovery, and reform.

FIRESIDE CHATS

Roosevelt's March 12 speech on banking was his first radio address as president, though he had used the format before as governor of New York. After he spoke to the national audience, these talks became known as fireside chats. The announcer who introduced Roosevelt on March 12 said, "The president wants to come into your home and sit at your fireside for a little chat," and the name stuck. The talks always began with the words "My friends" and lasted 15 minutes.

Relief for Those Who Needed It Most

Chapter

4

Correcting what was wrong with the economy was important to the country's long-term stability, as was regulating banking and big business. But Roosevelt also understood that ordinary Americans needed real help, and they needed it immediately. He began by focusing on the portion of the population that had been hit hardest by the Depression. He did this by using a system of programs designed to offer relief—the first *R* in the three R's of the New Deal.

During the first 100 days of Roosevelt's presidency, his administration created seven programs designed to provide economic—and emotional—relief to the millions of people who suffered during the Depression.

The Civilian Conservation Corps (CCC) was considered one of the most important New Deal programs. Created on March 31, 1933, this program had two basic goals: to provide jobs and training to unemployed men, and to conserve and develop the country's natural resources.

Members of the CCC were young men who worked to protect the country's land and natural resources.

Roosevelt had long been interested in protecting and improving the nation's natural resources. As governor of New York, he had employed 10,000 jobless men on conservation projects. Now, as president, he could combine two of his passions—finding jobs for the unemployed and improving natural resources—on a massive scale.

Some Americans were opposed to conservation programs, which they considered a form of charity. They argued that conservation projects were not jobs that were necessary. This was not the case, however, with the CCC. In addition to planting trees, fighting forest fires, and building roads, members of the CCC helped correct erosion problems and otherwise improve public lands.

CCC workers were paid to do all kinds of jobs, such as clearing rocks and snow from roads.

THE NEW BONUS EXPEDITIONARY FORCE

In the spring of 1933, a new Bonus Expeditionary Force made its way to Washington, D.C. Marchers hoped that the new president would be more sympathetic to their cause than Hoover had been. Though Roosevelt's answer was the same, his approach was very different. He sent his most trusted aide to make sure the marchers had three hot meals a day, and he allowed them to stay in the Army barracks near the Capitol. The first lady also visited the men and talked with them about their experiences during World War I. Though Roosevelt could not get them their bonuses—the government just did not have that much cash to spare—he did arrange for many of the men to get jobs through the CCC. Though the CCC age limit was 25, Roosevelt made sure that restriction was lifted for any veteran who wanted to join. More than 75 percent of the marchers who had traveled to Washington, D.C., took the president up on the offer.

Many of the unemployed youth of the country lived in the East, but most of the work that needed to be done lay in the western parts of the country. As a result, recruits frequently found themselves working far from home. They often lived in work camps that had been originally built as military camps for the War Department during World War I. Even so, young men were eager to sign up.

The CCC was open to men between the ages of 18 and 25 whose families were receiving state or local relief. These men were given free room and board and paid $30 per month, the equivalent of about $450 today. The men received $5 a month as spending money, while the other $25 was sent directly to their families back home.

45

The economic benefits of the CCC quickly became clear. Not only were these men providing income for their families, but they were also using their spending money to boost the economies of the towns in which they worked. CCC workers were probably responsible for saving many small businesses from ruin. The CCC also inspired the creation of other similar work programs.

The environmental benefits of the work completed through the CCC can be seen today in and around national and state parks and forests in the United States. During the program's existence,

A plaque commemorated the work of the CCC.

CIVILIAN CONSERVATION CORPS (C.C.C.)

THIS MEMORIAL IS DEDICATED TO ALL WHO SERVED IN ARIZONA AND THE THREE MILLION WHO SERVED IN THE C.C.C.'S NATIONWIDE.

"THE PRESIDENT'S TREE ARMY"
1933-1942

ERECTED BY THE CIVILIAN CONSERVATION CORPS ALUMNI OF ARIZONA

"IT WAS THE BEST THING THAT EVER HAPPENED TO ME"

CCC workers were responsible for building 97,000 miles (155,000 kilometers) of fire roads, erecting 3,470 fire towers, and spending a combined total of more than 4 million days fighting fires. They also planted more than 3 billion trees, stopped erosion on more than 20 million acres (8 million hectares) of land, and conducted countless other conservation projects.

In May 1933, Roosevelt's administration established the Federal Emergency Relief Administration (FERA) to assist those Americans who were not eligible for the CCC. Though FERA operated some smaller work projects, its main function was to supplement state welfare programs by giving money directly to people who needed it.

For every $3 a state spent on direct relief, the federal government contributed $1. A sum of $500 million was immediately set aside for the 6 million people on city and state relief lists and the 15 million people who were jobless. Over the next two years, federal and state governments spent a total of $3 billion through FERA.

The people who benefited most from the CCC and FERA were those who were living in the cities. But farmers were facing hard times as well. The first program designed specifically to give relief to this part of the population was the Emergency Farm Mortgage Act, which was also passed in May 1933.

All across the rural areas of the United States, farmers were losing their property because they could no longer afford their monthly mortgage payments. When a farm was in foreclosure, everything was taken from the farmer. Families lost their land, their homes, and even their livestock and machinery.

The bank that held the loan would sell everything on a farm at an auction. Some items were sold for just pennies. Whenever they could, a farmer's neighbors would try to buy the property back at auction and return it to the farmer. Unfortunately, few people had the money to help out. On other occasions, people took advantage of their neighbors' misfortune and used the opportunity to buy up cheap farm equipment for themselves.

The Depression was not the only thing hurting farmers in the United States. A seven-year drought that began in 1931 was followed by severe dust storms in the Great Plains in 1932. Much of the topsoil in parts of Kansas, Oklahoma, Colorado, and Texas dried up and was blown away.

With no farmland to till, hundreds of farmers packed up their families and their few possessions and headed to California. There, they hoped to find jobs as migrant workers. But Californians were struggling to find work, too, and the state already had a large population of migrant workers, mostly from Mexico. Many Midwestern farmers found themselves turned away at California's border.

The Emergency Farm Mortgage Act put a stop to foreclosures and helped farmers refinance their mortgages at lower rates, making them easier to pay off. The Farm Credit Act, which was passed on June 16, 1933, offered further relief to farmers in the form of generous refinancing options.

People from the Midwest who went to California were often left without jobs or homes.

49

Another program that benefited rural areas of the United States was the Tennessee Valley Authority (TVA), introduced by Nebraska Senator George Norris. The Tennessee River often flooded the lands surrounding it, causing soil erosion, which robbed the soil of important nutrients. The flooding and erosion made farming in the area difficult.

The purpose of the TVA was to control the river through the construction of dams. This would solve several problems for people living in the area. The dams would stop erosion caused by flooding, which would help restore fertility to the farmland. The dams would also produce cheap electricity for areas that up to that point had no electricity at all. The TVA would put young people to work building these dams and power plants.

Although some people wondered whether the country's tax money should be spent for the benefit of one relatively small area, Roosevelt and the Congress did not have any doubts. Approximately 40,000 men had been hired and $2 billion had been spent to build 20 new dams and improve those that already existed.

Thousands of people were able to get electricity at a reasonable price, and in the process, workers were able to develop and perfect new agricultural techniques. Workers rebuilt the land, planted trees, and learned to control soil erosion.

Eventually, they developed a program to teach other farmers throughout the country how to do the same. The money made from farming in the Tennessee Valley increased by 200 percent.

TVA workers built the Fort Loudon Dam in Lenoir, Tennessee.

51

From 1933 to 1936, former Associated Press journalist Lorena Hickok wrote field reports for the TVA. In her report from June 6, 1934, she observed:

> *I've talked with people who are doing this job, with people who live in the towns and cities that are going to feel the effects of this program, with ordinary citizens, with citizens on relief—as many kinds of people as I could find. ... Nearly 10,000 men ... are at work in the Valley now, at Norris and Wheeler dams, on various clearing and building projects all over the area.*

> *Thousands of them are residents of the Valley, working five-and-a-half hours a day, five days a week, for a really LIVING wage. Houses are going up for them to live in—better houses than they have ever had in their lives before. And in their leisure time they are studying— farming, trades, the art of living, preparing themselves for the fuller lives they are to lead in that Promised Land.*

> *And people say to you, 'Oh, we're lucky down here in Tennessee. TVA's a help!'*

> *'Oh, I haven't heard anybody say anything about the Depression for three months,' remarked a taxicab driver in Knoxville the other day. 'Business is three times as good as it was a year ago. You ought to see the crowds at the ballgames.'*

But the TVA eventually ran into opposition. It had become a major provider of inexpensive electricity in the United States, and private companies claimed unfair competition. They said that the federal government's involvement in the utilities business was unconstitutional. Years of court battles followed, but on February 17, 1936, the Supreme Court ultimately upheld the constitutionality of the act.

In June 1933, the U.S. Congress passed the Home Owners' Loan Corporation (HOLC) Act. Like the Emergency Farm Mortgage Act, HOLC helped homeowners who were in danger of losing their homes. In just one year, the government gave 300,000 loans to people in need.

These loans allowed people to pay off their mortgages over a longer period of time—and at a lower monthly payment rate. This program helped about 1 million Americans keep homes that they would otherwise have lost.

Little by little, the government was assisting its citizens. By addressing the peoples' most pressing concerns, such as finding jobs and keeping their homes, the New Deal policies were giving people a chance to improve their quality of life. ◣

COMPETING WITH THE GOVERNMENT

The private owners of U.S. utility companies did not like competing with the federal government for business. Because the TVA was a tax-funded relief program, the government could supply cheap electricity to people. There was no way the utility companies could compete at those prices, so they felt the government had an unfair advantage. They argued that it was illegal for the government to run this kind of business. But the Supreme Court said their argument was wrong.

The Road to Recovery

Helping individuals get back on their feet with relief programs was a step toward stimulating the country's economy. Larger measures would be needed, however, to achieve actual results, and that is where the second of the New Deal's three R's—recovery—came in. The purpose of the recovery programs was to restore the economy to pre-Depression levels.

The first of the New Deal recovery measures, the Emergency Banking Act, was actually put into place before any of the relief programs. During the bank holiday shortly after Roosevelt took office, Congress came up with a way to regulate the country's banking system. The Emergency Banking Act ensured that banks would reopen under strict government supervision. Among other things, that meant making sure that banks no longer made risky loans that had little chance of being paid back.

The act also gave the U.S. Treasury the power to issue more paper money and to prevent people from stockpiling gold. By making Americans return gold they were holding onto, the government was ensuring that people would have to place their trust in government-issued money.

The Bureau of Engraving and Printing in Washington, D.C., worked around the clock to produce more paper money for the United States.

Less than a month after banks reopened, more than a billion dollars in currency had returned to them. Americans had taken Roosevelt at his word: They knew that if they did not place their faith in the banking system, the economy could not recover.

In April 1933, Roosevelt took the United States off the gold standard. At that time, gold was the standard measure for all the world's currencies. For example, imagine that 1 ounce (28 grams) of gold equaled one American dollar, two British pounds, or three French francs. That would mean a person could buy an item that had a value of 1 ounce of gold in the United States, Great Britain, or France and be paying the same price. Being on the gold standard made it easier for nations to trade with one another. Countries did not actually pay each other in gold bars. Instead, they used paper currency—but that money was backed up by the corresponding amount of gold in a vault somewhere within their country.

The U.S. Treasury could not print a $20 bill unless the corresponding lump of gold was in reserve at one of the country's gold storage facilities. Today, these include Fort Knox in Kentucky, the West Point Bullion Depository in New York, and

GIVE BACK YOUR GOLD

On April 5, 1933, President Roosevelt signed an Executive Order that required anyone who still owned gold coins, bullion, or gold certificates worth more than $100 to trade them in for paper money. Exceptions were allowed for industrial use of gold and rare coins that were purchased as collectibles.

the United States Mint in Denver, Colorado. Having to have gold to back up paper money meant that when people held onto gold, paper money was scarce. When Roosevelt took the country off the gold standard and every dollar did not have to be backed in gold, the nation's ability to sell products around the world improved.

Two months later, Congress passed the Gold Clause Resolution. Until that time, all pubic or private contracts demanded that payment be made in gold or its equivalent. The resolution canceled that provision, making it the norm for payment to be made in paper currency.

On June 16, 1933, near the end of Roosevelt's historic first 100 days of lawmaking, the president introduced a program that he hoped would be the magic charm to end the Depression: the National Industrial Recovery Act, which set up the National Recovery Administration (NRA). Roosevelt said:

> *History will record the National Industrial Recovery Act as the most important and far-reaching legislation ever enacted by the American Congress. It represents a supreme effort to stabilize for all times the many factors which make for the prosperity of the nation and the preservation of American standards.*

At that time, workers were at the mercy of their employers, working as many hours for as much or as little money as their employer required. Workers who joined together in unions had more power to negotiate with employers. If a boss refused to pay one person a reasonable wage, for example, the entire union could go on strike, or stop working.

Labor strikes became a common sight in the 1930s.

CONSOLIDATED
CAFETERIA

58

The NRA recognized and strengthened labor unions by encouraging employers to negotiate issues such as salary and working conditions with unions rather than individual employees. The NRA also set a maximum number of hours that an employee could work and created a minimum wage.

The act also allowed for government-sponsored price fixing. For example, if the price of a loaf of bread was set at 5 cents, no company could decide to charge 4 cents. The idea was that preventing companies from undercutting each other's prices would keep smaller businesses from failing.

The government also controlled how much of each product each business could make. This kept prices at a reasonable level by preventing companies from flooding the market with their products. The NRA also sought to control unfair competition by controlling marketing. It prohibited false advertising and attacks on rival companies.

All of these actions seemed very unusual and controversial at the time. The government had never been deeply involved in the practices of individual businesses before. But an even more controversial part of the NRA prohibited industries from making any technical advances that would cause a company to lay off workers. In other words, if they invented a machine that could do the work of two men, they could not use it. This helped people keep their jobs, but it positioned the

Businesses showed their support for the NRA by displaying posters in their windows.

United States behind other countries in the global market. While other nations made advances in technology, American companies had to keep doing things the old way.

PROHIBITING PROHIBITION

The 18th Amendment to the U.S. Constitution prohibited the manufacture, sale, and possession of alcohol. It was ratified in January 1919. This law, however, was not very effective, and the illegal trade in alcohol and the establishments that served it flourished. Roosevelt proposed doing away with the law as another way to stimulate the economy. States that were not opposed to the sale and possession of liquor could earn tax money through liquor sales. On December 5, 1933, the 21st Amendment to the U.S. Constitution, repealing Prohibition, was ratified.

Not surprisingly, industry leaders did not like the NRA at all—and they did everything in their power to stop the program, including taking their case to the Supreme Court. Roosevelt's hopes for his program would not be fulfilled—the NRA did not ultimately end the Depression. ◣

Reforming the System

6

The third *R* in the New Deal was reform. Roosevelt felt that reforming the country's economic system would be essential to ending the Great Depression. More importantly, if they were done correctly, these reform programs would help ensure that the United States would not suffer another depression in the future.

Many people believed that an unstable market caused the Great Depression. During World War I and the boom that followed, production was at an all-time high. Soon supply exceeded demand. There was more corn than people needed, and cars kept being made even after most families already had one. The agricultural and other industries did not do anything to adjust their production to meet this lower demand.

Low prices caused by agricultural surpluses hurt American farmers and prompted government intervention.

THIS IS ONE OF THE
U.S. GOVERNMENT
SURPLUS FOODS

DRIED
PRUNES

LOW PRICE DUE TO ABUNDANT CROPS

17¢

of This Healthful Food
· · Good For Prosperity

U. S. GOVERNMENT
DESIGNATES

17 FOODS
AS
BIG BARGAINS

LOW PRICE DUE TO ABUNDANT CROPS

BUTTER   DRIED PRUNES
EGGS   FANCY RICE
LARD   DRIED RAISINS
DRIED BEANS   FRESH APPLES
CORN MEAL   FRESH GRAPEFRUIT
WHEAT FLOUR   FRESH ORANGES
GRAHAM FLOUR   FRESH PEARS
HOMINY GRITS   DRY ONIONS
        PORK - EXCEPT PREPARED

EAT MORE OF THESE WHOLESOME FOODS

ORANGE and BLUE
FOOD STAMPS
REDEEMED HERE

We are helping
FARMERS OF AMERICA
MOVE SURPLUS FOODS

CREAM CRACK

Farm prices plummeted so low that farmers were spending more money to grow crops than they made selling them. One day in 1933, Paul Angle, a man who lived in Illinois, part of an area called the Corn Belt, met up with a friend in the bank. He later recalled how that friend demonstrated how bad farm prices had gotten:

> *During our conversation he took a 50-cent piece from his pocket and threw it on one of the bank's glass-topped writing tables. 'Paul Angle,' he exclaimed, 'you're a sturdy fellow, but you can't carry out of this bank all the corn that half dollar will buy!' He was right: There are 56 pounds in a bushel of corn, and the price was then ten cents a bushel.*

In addition to farmers losing their income, many factory workers also lost their jobs. Many factories had to lay off workers or close their doors.

It seemed that the best way to get the economy back on its feet and keep it running smoothly was to thoroughly reform the system. The government stepped in and controlled the market enough so that the needs of farmers, businesses, and workers were all met.

The Emergency Farm Mortgage Act had helped individual farmers keep their land, but it did not correct the underlying problem that was facing the entire agricultural industry. For that, Congress passed the Agricultural Adjustment Act (AAA) in May 1933.

The intent of the law was to bring farm incomes back up to the levels that existed in 1914, the last time farmers had made a decent living. The AAA itself was specifically designed to balance supply and demand by controlling how much farmers produced every year. To keep track of this, agents from the Department of Agriculture were sent out to individual farms to see how much was being produced.

ALPHABET SOUP

So many of the New Deal programs were known only by their initials that they were eventually given the nickname "Alphabet Soup." They included the Agricultural Adjustment Act (AAA), the Civilian Conservation Corps (CCC), and the Tennessee Valley Authority (TVA).

In those cases where agents found over-production, farmers were paid to destroy their excess crops. The government spent $200 million to pay cotton farmers to plow under 10 million acres (4 million hectares) of "excess" cotton. In another instance, 6 million piglets were slaughtered rather than sent to market. The money to pay these farmers came from a tax that was placed on the processing companies that produced food and clothing from farm products.

People who were opposed to the AAA attacked Roosevelt for what they saw as a huge waste of resources. They could not understand why the government would throw away food when so many Americans were starving. What these critics failed to acknowledge was that the pork from the slaughtered animals was frozen and given to those in need through the government's Federal Surplus Relief Corporation. Though some crops were destroyed through the AAA, others were salvaged for the needy. After the Federal Surplus Relief Corporation removed surplus products from the market, it funneled them to state and local relief organizations. Those agencies, in turn, distributed the food to the needy in their areas.

For some people, bread lines offered their only source of food during the Depression.

Even if farmers and other critics did not like the idea of destroying crops rather than selling them, it was hard to argue with the results. In 1932, wheat had been selling for 38 cents per bushel, and by 1936, that price was up to $1.02 per bushel. Still, that same year, the Supreme Court declared that taxing one group—the processors—to pay another—the farmers—was unconstitutional. The AAA in its original form was defeated.

Later in May, Congress passed the Federal Securities Act, designed to regulate the stock market and prevent improper dealings. It required that investors be told everything about the stocks or bonds they were planning to purchase. Investors now had the right to know how the business operated, how much money it made, and how it planned to spend the money from the sale of the stock.

The act also required that all new stock issues be registered with the government before being offered to the public. This law would later be supplemented by the Securities Exchange Act in 1934.

In June 1933, Congress passed the Glass-Steagall Banking Act, which created the Federal Deposit Insurance Corporation (FDIC). For the first time ever, the money people deposited in the bank was insured by the government. Now, if a bank failed or was robbed, customers had the guarantee that they'd get their money back from the government. After it was enacted, the FDIC

Roosevelt's programs improved the lives of many during the Depression, including those of CCC members, who celebrated with the president in 1933.

covered $5,000 for each individual customer. That was a lot of money in the 1930s. Over the years, though, the coverage has been raised. The limit is currently $100,000 per depositor at each bank he or she uses.

The Glass-Steagall Bill also helped put an end to corruption in banking. The Great Depression was caused in part by banks investing depositors' money in risky stocks and making large loans to businesses without researching the business owners or their plans for the company. Thanks to the Glass-Steagall Bill, banks were no longer allowed to invest in stocks or untested business schemes.

At the end of Roosevelt's legendary first 100 days, the unemployment rate remained high and the Depression was far from over. But there was no doubt that the early New Deal programs had helped ease human suffering. Although people were still poor, many had jobs and more families were getting direct relief from the government. And though the first 100 days were past, Roosevelt would continue to develop more and more programs in his battle to pull the nation back from the brink of disaster. ◣

RIDING THE RAILS

On June 16, 1933, Congress passed the Emergency Railroad Transportation Act, which was intended to consolidate and reorganize the rail system in the United States. But, conflicts between all parties involved—stockholders, workers, management, and even cities—kept the program from making any progress. The major railroad lines were kept afloat by government loans until World War II created an upturn for the industry.

The Second New Deal

Chapter

7

By the beginning of 1934, Roosevelt's critics were growing in number and becoming more vocal. The president was faced with two distinctly different opponents. Some thought Roosevelt was not doing enough to pull the country out of its economic slump. Others, however, thought he was doing too much.

Those who thought Roosevelt was too aggressive felt he was turning into a socialist. There are many aspects to socialism, but the main component deals with the production and distribution of goods. The means for producing and distributing goods is either controlled by the society as a whole (instead of by a handful of individuals) or by a strong central government. Not surprisingly, this group of Roosevelt's critics was made up largely of wealthy businessmen.

They resented the fact that President Roosevelt's tight regulations on their businesses were costing them money.

The group that felt Roosevelt was doing too little included Upton Sinclair, author of *The Jungle*. His book exposed conditions in meat-packing plants in Chicago and led to changes in food laws in the United States. Sinclair felt that Roosevelt's programs were not doing enough to help people. He ran for governor of California with a plan, called End Poverty in California, that he claimed would totally eliminate poverty within four years.

Upton Sinclair had a bold plan for ending poverty in his home state of California.

The plan called for government ownership of factories and businesses. Foreclosed farms would be bought by the government and worked by farmers who had lost their property. The plan also called for a monthly pension for people over the age of 60. Following a dirty campaign run by his opponent, however, Sinclair lost his bid for governor.

In September 1934, Roosevelt gave a fireside chat in which he tried to appease both sides. For big businessmen who thought he was too controlling, Roosevelt assured them that he did not intend to do away with private ownership of businesses or get in the way of profit-making opportunities. For those who thought he had not done enough, the president promised more programs in the future.

Once again, Roosevelt followed up his words with action. On May 6, 1935, the government committed the largest amount of money ever given in peacetime when it introduced the Works Progress Administration (WPA). It had a budget of $4.8 billion.

The task of allocating this money fell to Roosevelt's trusted aide, Harry Hopkins. The two men had worked together for years and shared a similar philosophy about bringing aid to the needy. Hopkins once said:

> *Give a man a [handout] and you save his body and destroy his spirit. Give him a job and you save both body and spirit.*

Hopkins arranged jobs for millions of people—about 2 million per month, in fact. WPA workers built everything from airports and roads to hospitals and schools. Some of the program's more famous projects include the Triboro Bridge in New York, the Hoover Dam in Nevada, and the National Zoo in Washington, D.C. Under the Rural Electrification Administration in 1935, the WPA helped bring electricity to rural areas that had never had power before.

A truly groundbreaking element of the WPA was that it also found work for musicians, actors, writers, painters, and historians. Harry Hopkins believed everybody had the right to a job, and he put these people to work painting murals, writing histories, putting on plays, and photographing life across the United States.

CAPTURING A PIECE OF HISTORY

As part of the Writers' Project of the WPA, workers interviewed and photographed 2,300 former slaves in order to preserve their personal histories. The resulting book, *Born in Slavery: Slave Narratives from the Federal Writers' Project, 1936–1938*, offers a unique perspective on that shameful period in the country's past.

July 1935 saw passage of a landmark act that was considered a bill of rights for workers. The Wagner Act, or Labor Relations Act, banned any union that was formed by company management instead of actual workers. It also forbade any unfair practices like threats of job loss or blacklisting that kept workers from forming a union.

73

The WPA put artists to work creating sculptures and paintings for public buildings.

Roosevelt again took aim at the rich and powerful in 1935 when he signed into law the Public Utilities Holding Company Act. This law made it illegal for one huge company to control most of a public utility. He followed up this law with the Revenue Act of 1936, which allowed the government to claim up to 70 percent of large incomes in taxes.

PACKING THE COURT

On May 27, 1935, the big businesses that were opposed to the National Industrial Recovery Act finally won. The Supreme Court ruled that the act was unconstitutional. By the end of the year, there were hundreds of lawsuits against New Deal programs in the works. The president decided to try to influence the highest court in the land. In 1937, he proposed a bill that would allow him to appoint new judges when the older judges refused to retire. People referred to this plan as court packing, and no one, including Roosevelt's supporters, thought it was a good idea. Roosevelt gave up on his court-packing plan, but the Supreme Court justices got the message and stopped striking down the president's New Deal proposals. They were back in Roosevelt's corner.

Then, in the summer of 1935, Roosevelt signed the law he considered his administration's crowning achievement—the Social Security Act. Under this law, which is still in effect today, employers and employees contribute money every month to an "old-age" insurance fund. With Social Security in place, the American people no longer needed to worry about what would happen to them when they were too old to work. The act also provided for unemployment insurance, so that even young people who lost their jobs would not have to worry about going hungry while they looked for more work.

Roosevelt ran for president in 1936 against Republican opponent Alfred Landon. As the next election drew near, Republicans were quick to point out that after almost four years with the New Deal, the United States was still in a depression. That fact was clearly true. But Roosevelt argued that without his programs, things would have been worse. The numbers backed him up: When Roosevelt entered office, 12.8 million people were unemployed, but by 1936, that number had decreased to 9 million.

Alfred Landon, who served as governor of Kansas, ran against Roosevelt in the 1936 presidential election.

The American people agreed with their president, and Roosevelt won the 1936 election by a landslide, receiving 28 million votes to his opponent's 17 million. Things seemed to be looking up for the economy late in 1936, but by September of the next year, the United States was once again headed for a recession.

The Fair Labor and Standards Act signed in June 1938 was the last major reform law of the New Deal. It set the minimum wage at 40 cents per hour, limited the workweek to no more than 40 hours, and outlawed the hiring of children under the age of 16. It also dictated that workers younger than 18 could not be given dangerous jobs.

Like the other New Deal programs that ran from 1933 through 1938, this act had positive results. Unfortunately, however, none of them put a stop to the Depression. In the end, it would take nothing less than world war to get the U.S. economy back on its feet. ◣

The Great Arsenal of Democracy

While the United States had been struggling to get back on its feet financially, the rest of the world seemed to be descending further into chaos. Germany began recovering from its depression with a vengeance. German leader Adolf Hitler had been building up the country's military, and in 1936, he sent German troops into the Rhineland, the western part of Germany near France. Since the end of World War I, the Allied forces had occupied that area. Germany's military action went against the Treaty of Versailles, which Germany had signed at the end of World War I.

In Italy, dictator Benito Mussolini had sent his troops to invade the African country of Ethiopia. Meanwhile, Japanese forces were waging a bloody campaign for control of northern China.

Adolf Hitler used the depression in Germany to help him seize power for himself and his Nazi Party.

Over the next two years, German troops continued moving through Europe. They signed a "Pact of Steel" with Italy and invaded Poland in 1939. In response to that act of aggression, Great Britain and France declared war on Germany. Soon after, Canada would also declare war on Germany, but the United States stayed neutral. In fact, in 1936, President Roosevelt had said:

> *I hate war. I shall pass unnumbered hours, thinking and planning how war may be kept from this nation.*

President Roosevelt was also busy thinking about the upcoming 1940 election. Running for a third term was completely unheard of for a president. Although at the time there was no official limit to how many terms a president could serve, there was a long-standing tradition to not serve more than two terms. No other president in American history had ever run for a third straight term in office, and Republicans criticized the president for trying to break the two-term tradition.

SETTING THE LIMIT

There was no law saying a president could not run for more than two terms in office. But George Washington had started the tradition of a two-term limit during his presidency. Many Americans feared that a president who stayed in office too long could become too powerful and end up becoming a tyrant. After Roosevelt won a fourth term in 1944 and died while in office the following year, an amendment was added to the U.S. Constitution. The 22nd Amendment was ratified in 1947. It states that no one can be elected president more than twice.

But the American people had their own opinions. In early 1940, Germany had taken over Belgium, Denmark, Norway, and the Netherlands. Most people thought it was a bad time to change leadership. And so, once again, Roosevelt was elected president.

With the election behind him, Roosevelt shared more of his feelings about the war. Although he hoped not to engage the United States in actual battles, he would support Great Britain and France as much as possible. In September 1940, Roosevelt made a deal with Great Britain. The United States would supply warships to the Allies in exchange for leases to certain British military bases.

Then, in a December 29 fireside chat, the president spoke to the nation about the role of the United States in the war. He made it clear that it was time for the United States to do its part to defend democracy around the world. Americans would not be sent to fight, but weapons and munitions made in the United States would be sent to its Allies "swiftly and without stint." He said:

> *We must be the great arsenal of democracy. For us this is an emergency as serious as war itself. We must apply ourselves to our task with the same resolution, the same sense of urgency, the same spirit of patriotism and sacrifice as we would show were we at war.*

Roosevelt's generous offer to help the Allies would not only help Great Britain and France fight the war, but it would help the United States finally emerge from the Depression. The nation's industrial leaders responded to the president's call to action. Companies such as General Motors started making machine guns, and Chrysler built tanks. But even this huge surge in production did not turn things around immediately. By 1941, a year later, 10 percent of the nation's workforce was still unemployed.

The U.S. economy started to pick up as American factories began producing warplanes for the Allies in Europe.

That would change over the coming months, however. Before long, laborers were working at an incredible pace to build planes, warships, and tanks. More jobs were created as Army bases started appearing around the country to train young soldiers.

Then, on December 7, 1941, the Japanese navy attacked Pearl Harbor in Hawaii. With this attack, the United States became a full participant in World War II. The U.S. entry into the war was a turning point in the Great Depression—and in history.

Though it was the war and not New Deal programs that ultimately ended the Depression, the importance of President Roosevelt's programs and contributions cannot be understated. At the time, there were varied opinions as to how much Roosevelt's programs actually achieved and how well the president dealt with the Great Depression. In fact, the debate continues today.

Some feel the New Deal programs did not help enough people and that they created a huge national debt. Others point to the fates of other countries that were caught in the grip of depression including Russia, Italy, and Germany, where tyrants stripped people of their rights. They point out that Roosevelt helped the American people without taking away any of their freedoms. The New Deal did not end the Depression, but it helped preserve democracy in the United States.

Built by WPA workers, Nevada's Hoover Dam was one of many achievements of the New Deal programs that we continue to benefit from today.

84

The Great Depression was about more than the poverty of individual Americans. The very future of democracy was at stake. If the United States could not break out of its economic crisis, the country would be ripe for revolution and dictatorship. In fact, the two countries most affected by the global depression—Germany and the United States—went in opposite directions in response to the problem. Germany saw the rise of national socialism under the leadership of Adolf Hitler. In the United States, however, Franklin Delano Roosevelt worked to salvage and strengthen the democratic system of government.

The positive effects of the New Deal programs could be seen immediately in the 1930s. These programs saved the lives of millions of Americans who were penniless, starving, and homeless. They gave people a chance to get back on their feet. But many of its effects were even more far-reaching.

The New Deal redefined the role of the federal government in the lives of common people. The Roosevelt administration was the first to claim responsibility for the economic well-being of the country as a whole. This attitude, and indeed many of the original New Deal programs, continue to affect the lives of Americans today. They give Americans a sense of security and a quality of life that is constantly improving.

Thanks to Social Security, Americans have a financial cushion to help them through their later years in life. Unemployment insurance continues to provide a safety net for people who are between jobs. And people who place their life savings in the care of banks have the peace of mind that comes with knowing their money will still be there when they need it.

Without a doubt, the Great Depression was a terrible tragedy that left incredible economic and human devastation in its wake. But the government and nation that emerged from that crisis were stronger than ever before.

Timeline

1917–1918

The United States fights in World War I, which began in other countries in 1914.

June 28, 1919

The Treaty of Versailles is signed.

Summer 1921

Franklin Delano Roosevelt is stricken with polio.

November 7, 1928

Herbert Hoover is elected president.

October 1929

The stock market crashes.

1931

A severe drought hits the Great Plains.

February 2, 1932

The Reconstruction Finance Act is passed.

Summer 1932

The Bonus Expeditionary Force arrives in Washington, D.C.

July 2, 1932

Roosevelt wins the Democratic nomination for president and makes his "New Deal" speech.

November 8, 1932

Roosevelt is elected president.

1932

Dust storms in the Great Plains dry up the topsoil and carry it away, creating the Dust Bowl.

March 4, 1933

Roosevelt takes office and makes inaugural address.

March 6, 1933

Roosevelt declares a bank holiday and calls Congress into special session.

March 9, 1933

The Emergency Banking Relief Act is passed.

March 12, 1933

Roosevelt makes his first radio address as president to explain the banking crisis.

March 31, 1933

The Civilian Conservation Corps is created.

April 19, 1933

Roosevelt takes the United States off the gold standard and signs an Executive Order requiring citizens to trade in their gold for paper currency.

May 12, 1933

The Federal Emergency Relief Act is passed.

The Agricultural Adjustment Act is passed.

The Farm Relief Act is passed.

May 18, 1933

The Tennessee Valley Authority is established.

May 27, 1933

The Federal Securities Act is passed.

Spring 1933

The new Bonus Expeditionary Force returns to Washington, D.C.

June 13, 1933

The Home Owners' Loan Corporation Act is passed.

June 11, 1933

FDR completes his historic first 100 days in office.

June 16, 1933

The Glass-Steagall Banking Act is passed.

The National Industrial Recovery Act is passed.

The Emergency Railroad Transportation Act is passed.

The Farm Credit Act is passed.

December 5, 1933

The 21st Amendment repealing Prohibition is ratified.

January 31, 1934

Congress creates the Federal Farm Mortgage Corporation.

June 6, 1934

The Securities Exchange Act is passed.

June 28, 1934

The National Housing Act is passed to provide low-cost housing.

April 8, 1935

The Emergency Appropriations Relief Act is passed, creating the Works Progress Administration.

Timeline

May 11, 1935
The Rural Electrification Administration is established.

May 27, 1935
The Supreme Court declares the National Industrial Recovery Act unconstitutional.

July 5, 1935
The Wagner Act is passed.

August 14, 1935
The Social Security Act is passed.

August 28, 1935
 The Public Utilities Holding Company Act is passed.

Spring 1936
Adolf Hitler begins to move through Europe; Benito Mussolini invades Ethiopia; Japan moves through China.

November 3, 1936
Roosevelt is elected to his second term as president.

June 25, 1938
The Fair Labor and Standards Act is signed.

Spring 1939
Germany and Italy sign "Pact of Steel"; Germany invades Poland; Great Britain and France declare war on Germany.

September 1940
Roosevelt agrees to supply destroyers to the Allies.

November 7, 1940
Roosevelt wins his third term in office, defeating Wendell Willkie.

December 29, 1940
Roosevelt gives a fireside chat in which he declares the United States the "great arsenal of democracy."

December 7, 1941
Japan attacks Pearl Harbor; the United States enters World War II.

ON THE WEB

For more information on *The New Deal*, use FactHound.

1 Go to *www.facthound.com*

2 Type in this book ID: 0756520967

3 Click on the *Fetch It* button. FactHound will find Web sites related to this book.

HISTORIC SITES

Home of Franklin D. Roosevelt
4097 Albany Post Road
Hyde Park, NY 12538
845/229-9115

Visitors may tour Roosevelt's home, which includes his presidential library and museum.

The Hoover Dam in Nevada
Mendocino Woodlands State Park in California
The National Zoo in Washington, D.C.

Visitors can see some of the more famous public works projects completed as a result of the New Deal.

LOOK FOR MORE BOOKS IN THIS SERIES

The Collapse of the Soviet Union:
The End of an Empire
ISBN 0-7565-2009-6

McCarthyism:
The Red Scare
ISBN 0-7565-2007-X

Hurricane Katrina:
Afternmath of Disaster
ISBN 0-7565-2101-7

Miranda v. Arizona:
The Rights of the Accused
ISBN 0-7565-2008-8

The Little Rock Nine:
Struggle for Integration
ISBN 0-7565-2011-8

Watergate:
Scandal in the White House
ISBN 0-7565-2010-X

A complete list of **Snapshots in History** titles is available on our Web site: *www.compasspointbooks.com*

Glossary

arsenal
place where arms and other military equipment are manufactured and/or stored

blacklisting
when a person is placed on a list of people to be punished

controversial
something that causes dispute

crusade
mission that is undertaken with great passion

exports
products that are made in one country for sale to other countries

grueling
very difficult or taxing

inauguration
the ceremony where the president is formally inducted into office

isolationist
policy in which one country does not get involved with the political, social, or economic affairs of other countries

mandate
a command

memorabilia
personal mementos

migrant
person who moves regularly to find work

plummeted
dropped or declined sharply

ratified
signed or gave formal consent to; approved

recession
period marked by declining economic activity

unethical
action that does not live up to accepted standards of behavior

veteran
person who served in the armed forces

Source Notes

Chapter 1

Page 10, line 5: Franklin D. Roosevelt. "Inaugural Address, March 4, 1933." 4 March 1933. *New Deal Network*. 21 April 2006. http://newdeal. feri.org/speeches/1933a.htm

Chapter 2

Page 25, line 13: Studs Terkel. *Hard Times: An Oral History of the Great Depression*. New York: New Press, 1970, p. 46.

Page 27, line 20: Anne E. Schraff. *The Great Depression and the New Deal: America's Economic Collapse and Recovery*. New York: Franklin Watts, 1990, p. 22.

Chapter 3

Page 32, line 9: *The Great Depression and the New Deal: America's Economic Collapse and Recovery*, p. 43.

Page 36, line 3: Franklin D. Roosevelt. "Roosevelt's Nomination Address, 1932." 2 July 1932. *New Deal Network*. 21 April 2006. http://newdeal.feri. org/texts/61.htm

Page 40, line 3: Franklin D. Roosevelt. "On the Bank Crisis, March 12, 1933." 12 March 1933. *New Deal Network*. 21 April 2006. http://newdeal. feri.org/texts/379.htm

Page 41, sidebar: Kenneth Davis. *FDR: The New Deal Years 1933–1937: A History*. New York: Random House, 1986, p.60.

Chapter 4

Page 52, line 5: Lorena Hickok. "Letters from the Field." 6 June 1934. *New Deal Network*. 21 April 2006. http://newdeal.feri.org/tva/tva04.htm

Chapter 5

Page 57, line 20: *The Great Depression and the New Deal: America's Economic Collapse and Recovery*, p. 63.

SOURCE NOTES

Chapter 6

Page 64, line 8: David Colbert, ed. *Eyewitness to America: 500 Years of America in the Words of Those Who Saw It Happen.* New York: Pantheon Books, 1997, p. 378.

Chapter 7

Page 72, line 27: "Works Progress Administration." *PBS: The American Experience.* 21 April 2006. www.pbs.org/wgbh/amex/dustbowl/peopleevents/pandeAMEX10.html

Chapter 8

Page 80, line 9: James T. Patterson. *America in the Twentieth Century: A History.* Fort Worth, Texas: Harcourt College Publishers, 1999, p. 272.

Page 81, line 23: Franklin Delano Roosevelt. "The Great Arsenal of Democracy." Radio address. 29 Dec. 1940. *American Rhetoric.* 4 June 2006. www.americanrhetoric.com/speeches/fdrarsenalofdemocracy.html

SELECT BIBLIOGRAPHY

Colbert, David, ed. *Eyewitness to America: 500 Years of America in the Words of Those Who Saw It Happen.* New York: Pantheon Books, 1997.

Davis, Kenneth. *FDR: The New Deal Years 1933–1937: A History.* New York: Random House, 1986.

Patterson, James T. *America in the Twentieth Century: A History.* Fort Worth, Texas: Harcourt College Publishers, 1999.

Terkel, Studs. *Hard Times: An Oral History of the Great Depression.* New York: New Press, 1970.

FURTHER READING

Farrell, Jacqueline. *The Great Depression.* San Diego: Lucent Books, 1996.

Fremon, David K. *The Great Depression in American History.* Springfield, N.J.: Enslow Publishers, Inc., 1997.

Katz, William Loren. *The New Freedom to the New Deal, 1913–1939.* Austin, Texas: Raintree Steck-Vaughn, 1993.

Nishi, Dennis. *Life During the Great Depression.* San Diego: Lucent Books, 1998.

Schraff, Anne E. *The Great Depression and the New Deal: America's Economic Collapse and Recovery.* New York: Franklin Watts, 1990.

Stein, R. Conrad. *The Great Depression.* Chicago: Childrens Press, 1993.

Stewart, Gail B. *The New Deal.* New York: New Discovery Books, 1993.

Index

ABOUT THE AUTHOR

Stephanie Fitzgerald has been writing nonfiction for children for more than 10 years. Her specialties include history, wildlife, and popular culture. Stephanie lives in Stamford, Connecticut.

IMAGE CREDITS